designing
with letters

The Lettering Workbook series comprises:

Volume 1 **Basic skills**	ISBN 0-289-80013-7
Volume 2 **Traditional penmanship**	ISBN 0-289-80015-3
Volume 3 **Applied lettering**	ISBN 0-289-80014-5
Volume 4 **Designing with letters**	ISBN 0-289-80016-1

LETTERING WORKBOOKS

designing with letters

BRUCE ROBERTSON

STUDIO VISTA

Studio Vista
© Diagram Visual Information Ltd 1988

First published in Great Britain in 1989
by Studio Vista
an imprint of Cassell Publishers Limited
Artillery House, Artillery Row
London SW1P 1RT

British Library Cataloguing in Publication Data
Robertson, Bruce
    Designing with letters.–(Lettering workbooks)
    1. Lettering and design
    I. Title II. Series
    745.6'197

ISBN 0–289–80016–1

The Diagram Group

Designer	Bruce Robertson
Editor	Randal Gray
American consultant	Marian Appellof
Art staff	Elizabeth Benn, Brian Hewson, Bryan John, Lee Lawrence, Darren Maryon, Paul McCauley, Philip Patenall, Jane Robertson, Katherine Rubidge, Stuart Scott

Acknowledgements
We would like to thank Alianza Editorial
SA of Madrid, Spain, for permission to use
in this book several images from Enric
Satué's *El diseño gráfico desde los orígines
hasta nuestros días* (1988).
In the world of ephemeral printing many
designs appear without full credit either to
the designer, the company responsible for
the design, the date, or the current owners
of the copyright.
We have made every effort to locate and
clear permission for the use of the
illustrations in this book. But should we
have unwittingly infringed copyright in any
illustration reproduced we will gladly pay
an appropriate fee on being satisfied as to
the owner's title.

Printed and bound by Snoeck Ducaju & Sons,
Ghent, Belgium

Lettering Workbooks

THIS BOOK IS WRITTEN TO BE USED.
It is not meant to be simply read and
enjoyed. Like a course in physical exercises,
or any area of study, you must carry out
the tasks to gain benefit from the
instruction.

1 Read the book through once.
2 Begin again, reading two pages at a
   time and carry out the tasks set before
   you go on to the next two pages.
3 Review each chapter by re-examining
   your previous results and carrying out
   the review tasks.
4 Collect all your work and store it in a
   safe place, having written in pencil the
   date when you did the work.

LEARNING HOW TO DO THE TASKS IS NOT
THE OBJECT OF THE BOOK. It is to learn
lettering and calligraphy by practicing the
tasks. Do not rush them.

LETTERING WORKBOOKS ARE:
1 A program of clear instruction.
2 A practical account of various
   techniques and procedures.

Like a language course, the success of your
efforts depends upon you.
YOU DO THE WORK!

Contents

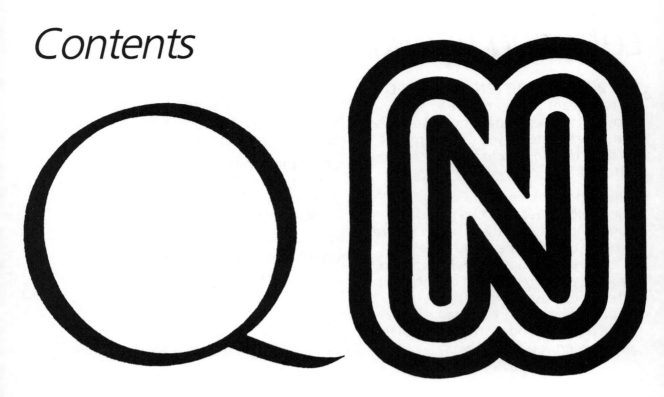

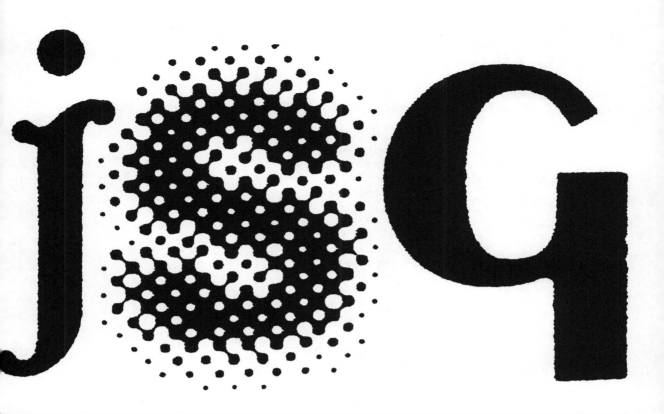

Topic finder

Introduction

This workbook serves as a guide to the enormous variety of alphabet and word designs created by designers over the past 5000 years. Because the more recent solutions appear predominantly in the ephemeral medium of print, the most interesting examples are often the work of unknown or forgotten artists. Nevertheless modern designers very much benefit from exposure to new ideas, or more importantly old ideas re-discovered. Designing is not a private or solitary activity, it is the resolving of visual problems for specific needs and, more likely, commercial demands. The creative designer is always at the service of his client. Twentieth century designers have paid greater attention to devising geometric forms than to traditional calligraphic ones. This is primarily because the newly designed letters are intended for duplication by artists who will simply repeat the methods of construction to arrive at the new forms. Calligraphic styles require intuitive writing skills that stem from much practice and knowledge. These skills are rarely taught satisfactorily today and in the current commercial world of design are bypassed in favor of more expedient methods such as dry transfer lettering.

There are a vast number of alphabet designs and many more interesting ways of organizing these into words. The success of a design can only be judged by the resulting word patterns, by the character of the projected word, its appropriateness, and its legibility. It is important to remember that, although words are made of letters, a newly designed word is more than the sum of its letters. The word has its own character and the best designers modify the arrangement both with care for spacing and with adjustments to individual letters.

The tasks and examples of exploratory designs in this book are those produced by students during my years as a lecturer in design. I always found that the uninitiated mind was the most creative when offered the challenge of thinking along new lines. Each person has some unique qualities to bring to design tasks, and no two designers offer similar solutions. The best designs are often those which are the product of fun, spontaneity and a willingness to look carefully and afresh at the shapes of letters and words.

Chapter 1

Origins

The original letters of our alphabet were written in lines of text that could be read along alternate lines in either directions. This *boustrophedon* style (the Ancient Greek for "ploughed field") in the example *(below)*, from a Lemnos column of c630 BC, enabled the scribe to write the first line from left to right, the second from right to left and so on through the text. This technique meant that vertically symmetrical letters like A M O were read the same in either direction, but vertically asymmetrical letters like E P Z appeared as mirror images of themselves in alternate lines.

Profusions

Five thousand years since the earliest letters were developed, the designer can incorporate an infinite variety of letter forms. *(Below)* An Italian 1915 designer, Ardenyo Soffici, plays with a futurist poem's letters using a technique known as collage (the sticking together of pieces of earlier printed materials).

LETTERS

Lettering is the visual form of speech. It uses symbols to represent sounds which in turn represent, when combined into groups to form words, the meanings and ideas we wish to convey. The symbols of the Western "Latin" alphabet have evolved over the past 5000 years. Although everyone agrees that these are the norm for the shape of each letter, their shapes can be subjected to an infinite variety of adaptations. The letters project their character, but must remain legible. They are the clothes that words wear. The skill of the lettering artist is an important feature of 20th century communication industries. Even with the growth over the past 80-90 years of cinema, radio and television, the printed and displayed word is still a strong contender for our attention. It is the most convenient method used in our streets, transportation systems, newspapers, magazines and books. Commercial pressures to seek attention for products have created a generation of inventive and imaginative designers who are pushing the letter shapes into ever wilder contortions. Traditional calligraphic forms are becoming extinct as computer technology enables designers to achieve distortions without having to master drawing skills.

Perversions
Letters convey meaning in their assembled groups of words. Here *(right)* Paul (an antique dealer) has designed his shopfront using classical Roman capital letters. He knows that in Roman times the letter U did not exist so he has inserted a V. The ultimate in perversion is to have put his telephone number GUL 3081 into Roman numerals!

Illegibility
This 1900 German designer has had fun inventing wildly distorted versions of letters *(right)*. The first word is ARCHITEKTUR, but subsequent words are extremely difficult to interpret. Remember that all designs however interesting must be legible.

PAVLS

II

GVL.
MMMLXXXI

Recognizing letters

After mastering the identification of letters in our early days at school we quickly become able to see the meaning of letters in many guises. Designers use this familiarity to play games with our perceptions and explore the letterforms as a means of conveying some special feature of the word.

Letter parts
Each letter's elements build up a construction which enables us to identify it and read the word in which it appears (*above*). The 1917 Dutch designer Theo Van Doesburg has devised elements to the letters within the words DE STYL that make it extremely hard for us to read the words. Legibility must always influence your strongest enthusiasm for new forms.

Parts of letters
Each letter is a group of marks distinguishable from the others by some unique feature. Several letters need only small adjustments to make similar ones: E is F with an added lower horizontal, R is P with an added diagonal. The examples (*below*) help one appreciate the uniqueness of letters. There are four alphabets drawn upside down in which only one half of a letter, either a vertical or horizontal section, is revealed. This proves that letters are so individual that no part can be misinterpreted; others could be misconstrued if only parts are revealed.

Letter shapes
The characters' shapes in MEXICO 68 (*above*) have been used to send vibrations across the surface like ripples caused by a stone thrown in a pond. Very few of the lines in this design form letters of the alphabet, but their overall impression suggests to us the Olympics word and date.

a   bhij   ceoq   ft   s   t   vwy   z   x
klmn
pr

The shape of space

Letters appear in groups, and the shapes they make between one another are often clues to their identification. Some produce similar shapes, others unique ones. The example (*above*) is of the shapes created between the lower case alphabet and a preceding vertical character.

Task
The shape of space

Place tracing paper over a large word or group of letters and, using a soft pencil or felt tip pen, fill in the spaces between the letters.

Variety

Although each letter has its own unique form, each can be portrayed in an infinite variety of styles (*above top*). The style of a letter is its current personality.

Task
Variety

Using a scrapbook containing over 26 pages, allocate a page or pages to a letter of the alphabet. Then stick examples of individual letters cut from as wide a source of printed material as you can find. You will quickly realize that this task has no end as there is an infinite number of letter variants.

Task
Shape recognition

Draw out the alphabet in capitals or lower case, or choose a simple word to draw. Use a thick felt tip pen, and draw the letters between two parallel pencil lines *upside down*. Then as a further experiment draw them back to front, and, even more challengingly, upside down and back to front.

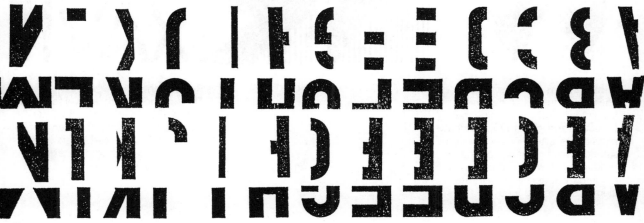

The shape of space

When we look at the shapes of letters it is often the surrounding shapes we also take into our impression that helps us identify the forms. Letters are traditionally seen as dark marks on a light background, but designers enjoy the playfulness of transposing the emphasis to a negative form, or omitting parts of the characters altogether.

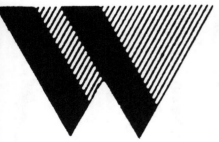

Solid or hollow
Letters can be solid dark areas, light areas on dark background, or described in outline (*above*) with their forms containing the same tonal value as the background.

Solid space
Because of our prejudgement of shapes (we expect the shapes to convey a message) designers can present the spaces between the words as the positive values (*left*), and leave us to read the message in the negative (omitted) values.

Ghosts
The three dimensional features of this example (*left*) leave us with the problem of reading into the spaces letters of the alphabet. Our familiarity with such letterform designs means that designers can mischievously hint at the letters.

Substitutions
The wonderful French designer Cassandre produced an alphabet (selection *above*) in 1929 that omitted parts of the letters. As each design solution was a carefully considered product, we have no difficulties in reading the letters as if their total elements were included.

Reflection
The strange pattern (*above*) forms the letters of the name XAVIER written twice, once normally and then as if in a mirror. How we read letters very much depends on what we expect them to say.

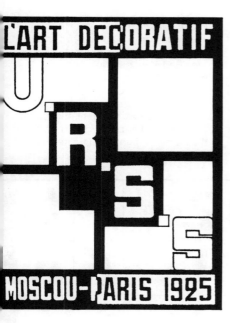

Negative and positive

This Alexander Rodchenko Soviet catalog cover of 1925 places the figures on light and dark backgrounds. The central figures URSS are both in outline and light on dark. A defect of this style of interchanging backgrounds is that the readers must change their reading methods within one statement.

Patterns

In the Islamic faith sentences from the Koran are so familiar that the designer of a quotation can play fantastic tricks with the shapes. The decorative labyrinth (*above right*) is not symmetrical as each of the eight segments contains different words in a greatly stylized version of Arabic script.

Visual clues

The designer of this 1968 advertisement and logo, Rosmari Tissi of Zurich, has played a trick on our perception of the letters by placing an absent letter P over the darker letters of T I and S. We read the P as pieces omitted from the other letters.

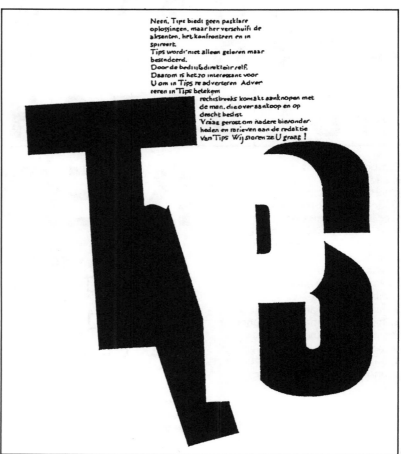

The growth of letters

Our current alphabet is the result of developments in the ancient civilizations of the Mediterranean. Prior to the single letters writing had often been an arrangement of simplified pictures (pictograms) used to express ideas and subjects. These first writing systems were slow to develop; they were difficult to implement as the scribe had to draw complex arrangements of lines for each "word."

Pictures as words

The visual form of an idea has to be simplified so that it can more easily be repeated in manuscripts and monuments. The name of the Egyptian Queen CLEOPATRA when written in our script contains nine letters. When written in hieroglyphics, the writing of ancient Egypt (*right*), the name contains 18 simplified pictures.

Symbols and signs

In addition to the commonly used letters, abbreviations of groups of letters or specific meanings have special letterforms (see *right*):

1 In German this is the mark for the two letters S and H when combined in a word.

2 In classically derived words (often in zoology or botany) this is the mark combining a and e.

3 This is Norwegian for double o.

4 This is the international symbol for the word AND, known as an ampersand.

5, 6 The common signs for the pound sterling and the dollar.

Noisy letters

The different European nations all use the same group of letters of the alphabet, but, to make the pronunciation intended clearer, the letters often carry additional marks to soften, harden, shorten or lengthen the sound (see *above*).

Roots

The chart (*below*) is based upon the work of the great lettering historian David Diringer. Each of the horizontal rows is from a different Mediterranean culture. Reading vertically Diringer suggests these indicate the development of the individual letterforms.

1 Phoenician
2 Classical Greek
3 Etruscan
4 Roman (Latin)
5 Modern Capitals

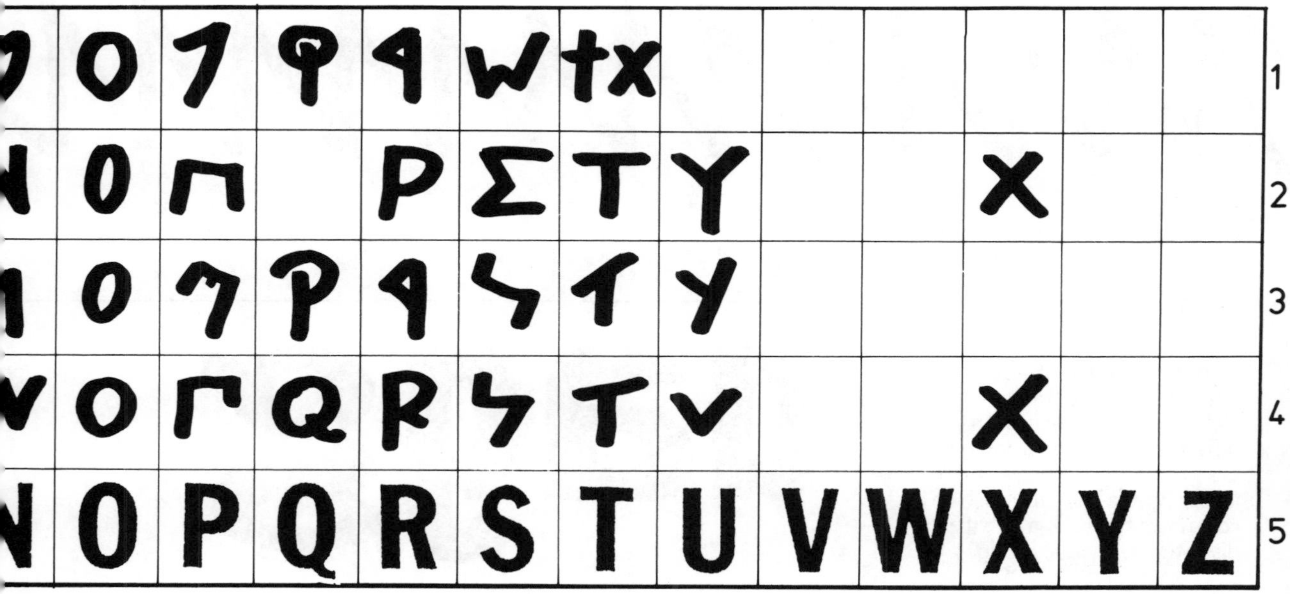

1
2
3
4
N O P Q R S T U V W X Y Z
5

Аа	Бб	Вв	Гг	Дд
Ее	Жж	Зз	Ии	
Кк	Лл	Мм	Нн	
Оо	Пп	Рр	Сс	Тт
Уу	Фф	Хх	Цц	Чч
Шш	Щщ	Ъъ	Ыы	
Ьь	Ээ	Юю	Яя	

Αα	Ββ	Γγ	Δδ
Εε	Ζζ	Ηη	Θϑ
Ιι	Κκ	Λλ	Μμ
Νν	Ξξ	Οο	Ππ
Ρρ	Σσς	Ττ	Υυ
Φφ	Χχ	Ψψ	Ωω

Other roots

Our present alphabet is one of a group of letterforms currently in use in Europe. Both the Greek alphabet (*left*) and the Russian, Cyrillic (*far left*) have a number of common letters, but they also include letter shapes unique to their languages.

Task

Signs and symbols

Copy out unfamiliar symbols from books and magazines. These are particularly common in books on mathematics, physics and geometry.

Elements of letters 1

Letters are an arrangement of linear parts, either straight or curved. Most have two basic forms, the larger forms (capital letters) and the smaller forms (lower case letters). Of the 26 letters of the alphabet 10 have the same form in both styles. These are C O P S U V W X Y Z. With these 10 common forms and the other 16 letters each with two forms the alphabet consists of 42 characters.

In addition two of the letters in the lower case have alternative forms; these are the a and the g. These characters, although complying to the accepted arrangement of shapes, can be subject to a wide variety of distortions. Their proportions, their elements, and the method of producing them can each influence their overall shapes.

Individuality
Groups of letters with common features when placed together can be difficult to read. The design (*above*) of seven letters in the lower case produces the English word minimum, which is hard to read as all its components have similar features.

Variations in the shapes
Two letters in the small versions of the alphabet (the lower case) have two different forms. The a and g can be drawn in different ways. All the other letters have a basic form which is consistent however much it is distorted by stylistic changes.

Variations in style
Because of the consistency of letter structure the designer can play tricks and design an alphabet in which the forms are pushed and distorted to points almost beyond recognition. The examples (*right*) show how different these solutions can be.

Variations in proportion
Letters may have normal ratios of height to width, or they may be greatly narrowed (condensed) or widened (extended).

1 ILHTEF

2 RPBJUD

3 KVXYZWMNA

4 OQCGS

Common components
The letters of the capital alphabet can be grouped into four types.
1 Those constructed from vertical and horizontal straight lines.
2 Letters made from combinations of straight and curved lines.
3 Those constructed from either vertical and diagonal lines combined or groups of diagonal lines.
4 Letters constructed from curves.

a 1 abcdefghij ABCDEF

b 1 abcdefgh ABCDEF

c 1 abcdefgh ABCDEFG

Heads, hands and feet
The ends of the letterforms can have a variety of design solutions.
a Traditional forms have tails (called serifs) which are the result of earlier forms produced by carving and calligraphy.
b The 19th century solutions often had very heavy mannered ends known collectively as Egyptian or Old Style serifs.
c Recent forms are without decorative ends and are known as Sans Serif.

©DIAGRAM

Elements of letters 2

The lower case letters have developed from a handwritten form. They are mostly made of curves and protruding verticals. The examples on these two pages are experiments by students creating letterforms from a small group of common elements.

Letter groups
The lower case letters can be arranged in three groups.
1 The central part falls between two common lines.
2 The letters have a vertical which extends (known as an ascender).
3 The letters have an element which protrudes (known as a descender) below the common area.

1

aceimnorsuvwxz

2

bdfhklt

3

gjpqy

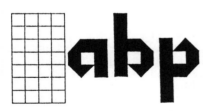

Task
Building blocks
Draw a grid of squares, four wide by seven deep. On a tracing paper overlay copy out each letter of the lower case alphabet, plotting the shapes within the grid. Make one square the width of all the elements and try to keep each letter's shape within the squares.

2

3

abcdefghijklm

4

abcdefghijklm

20

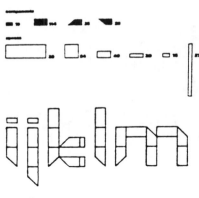

1

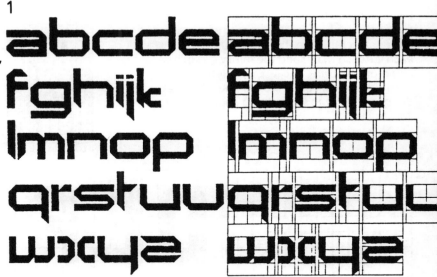

Building blocks

The smaller the individual parts of the construction are, the closer to the normal letter shapes they can be. The example (*right*) was made using only rectangles and triangles. The larger the elements the more ingenious and bizarre are the results (*below*).
Smaller elements **1, 3**
Larger elements **2, 4**

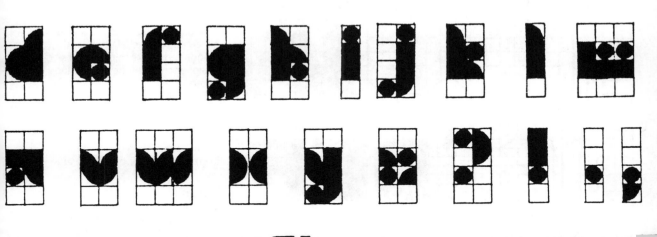

Matrix and modular

Contemporary forms of letters are often produced by the assembly of small elements within a grid or matrix. This regular net of lines is used to construct each letter so that it and the family group have a common structure. Because each letter's form is an assembly of small parts the ultimate alphabet design stems from the formula applied to their construction.

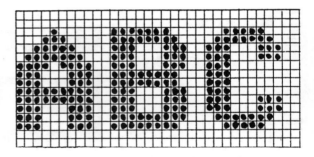

Task
Assembled form
The three letters (*above*) and the alphabet (*top right*) are the result of filling in squares on a regular grid. Using graph paper, build up the letters of a simple word by filling in dots on a square grid. The example shown uses a three-dot vertical stroke width and a two-dot horizontal stroke width. Diagonal lines and curves have to be expressed as stepped units.

Unit proportions
The examples (*left*) show how, by changing the number of squares allocated to the character widths, height and stroke thickness, the designer changes the style of the letters.
a 3 × 5 units, with one unit width for all strokes.
b 5 × 10 units, with two units width for all strokes.
c 6 × 7 units, with one unit for horizontals and two for verticals.

Task
Grid distortions
Using graph paper containing triangles construct a word or alphabet by the same method as the task above.

Electronic units
The letters (*left*) are designed for digital dials for clocks and meters. Each letter is made from a selection of the common part of a grid of verticals and horizontals. This method enables the electronic instructions to change the letters simply by changing the areas to be filled in.

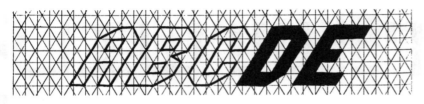

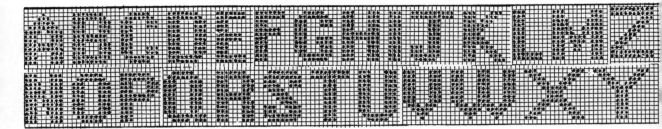

Industrial applications

The needlework pattern sheet (detail *right*) has converted the flowing calligraphic forms into an assembly of small units. When implemented the visual effect of the assembly of small points creates an illusion of a continuous smooth line.

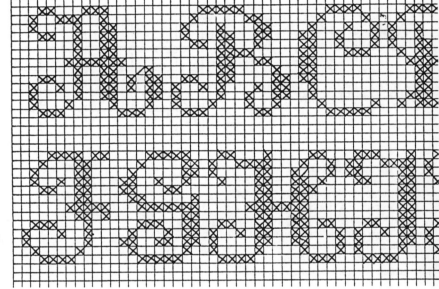

Computer forms

The VDU of a computer, and the dot matrix printer of a word processor achieve their visual effects by the same method as the embroiderer. Each letter is an assembly of very small units called Pixcels. The letter n (*right*) when seen actual size appears to be a smooth cursive line. This enlargement reveals the matrix structure of assembled tiny points.

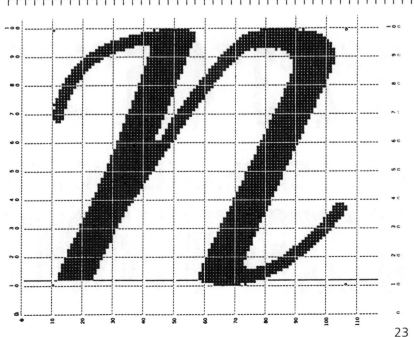

23

Regular distortion

If we consider that the letters can be constructed within regular grids, and assembled within a framework, we can then develop distortions of the letters by changing one or more of the ratios of the sides of the matrix. This method is very easy to draw and can also be applied to other alphabets which have calligraphic origins or traditional forms. The recent technology of word processors and computers has enabled typesetters simply to program their machines to produce distortions electronically.

Task
Regular distortion
Trace a simple word onto a regular grid (see *right*) (**A**) Redraw the grid changing one of the features, either condensed (**B**) or angular (**C**).

Constructed distortion
The example (*below*) is by a student who placed a fine grid over each of the letters of a standard alphabet and Arabic cardinal numbers, then, after vertically extending a similar grid, replotted the letters and figures so that their horizontal features remain constant but their vertical features become elongated.

B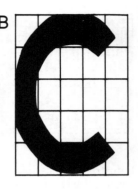

A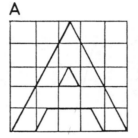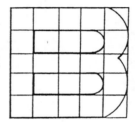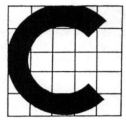

C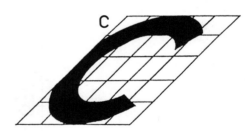

11 22 33 4 4 55 66 77 88 99 00

ABCDEFGHIJKLMNOPQRSTUVWXYZ

ABCDEFGHIJKLMNOPQRSTUVWXYZ

Ratio distortions
The most common method of changing the letter shapes is by extending the vertical or horizontal ratios and retaining all the other elements. This produces condensed (narrow) letters or expanded (widened) letters.

Angular distortions
Retaining the horizontal elements and constructing the vertical features at an angle to the horizontal produces sloping letters. This sloping to the right is commonly called Italic. A less common distortion is to retain the verticals and slope the horizontals.

Weight distortions
The ratio of the thickness within the letters to their overall proportions can be varied to create letters with thicker limbs (bold alphabets) or with thinner limbs (light alphabets).

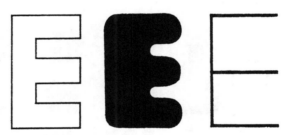

Emphasis distortions
Traditional calligraphic forms had thick and thin elements in the letter shapes which were the consequence of holding the broad-nibbed pen at a constant angle. Later designers used this feature to distort regular forms by systematically thickening either the vertical or the horizontal elements.

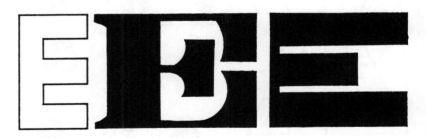

abcdefghijklmnopqrstuvwxyz

abcdefghijklmnopqrstuvwxyz

Irregular distortion

Letters are so commonly used in our everyday world that their forms have become recognizable even when subjected to the wildest distortions. A word printed on a balloon will change its shape when the surface is enlarged by inflating the balloon. Reflections of words in convex or concave mirrors take on unusual shapes like those seen in a fairground Hall of Mirrors. You can produce your own unique distortions by simply replotting a regular alphabet or word in an unusually distorted grid.

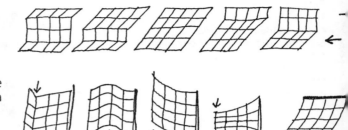

Inflatable distortions
The letters T A P (*left*) have been transformed by replotting on a surface which appears to be seen in a reflective sphere.

Task
Distortions
Select a style of grid from the examples above. Using a ruler and set square (triangle) or curves, construct a grid 2in (50mm) high. Draw some distorted letterforms.

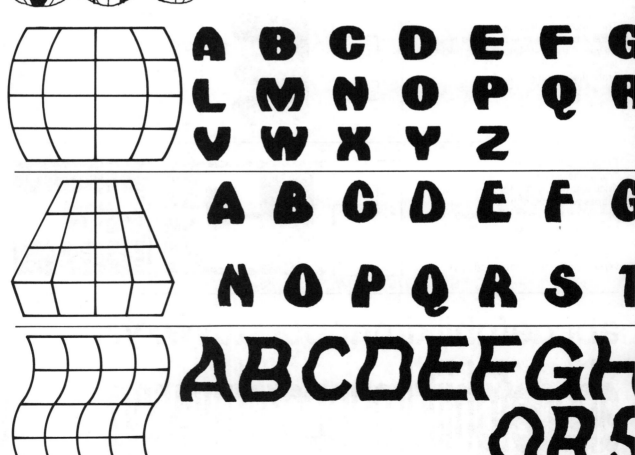

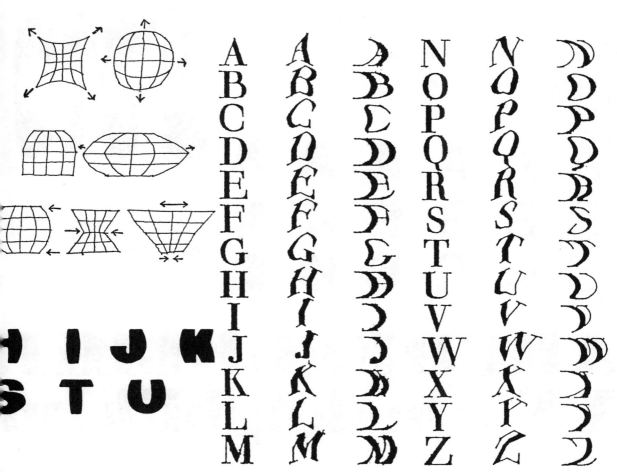

Geomorphic distortions

The three alphabets (*left*) were produced by students who replotted existing alphabets onto grids inspired by cartographic projections. When completed and the grid removed, the new alphabet often resembles forms produced by inflation or liquid distortions. The example (*below left*) twists a popular letterform to such an extent that its original character is hard to recognize.

Distortion by weight

Letters in their simplest form are thin line structures, but because of their calligraphic origins these lines are often expressed as thicks and thins. These variations in the linear forms have encouraged designers to explore the effects of distorting the letters by greatly varying the weights of parts of the letters.

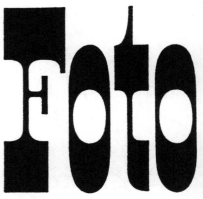

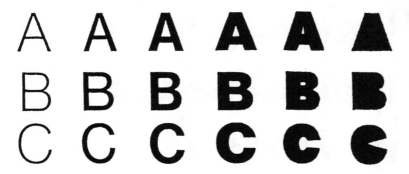

Stretch
The word foto (*above*) has had its vertical axis stretched resulting in a thickening of the horizontals.

Normal to abnormal
The three letters (*left*) are drawn in fine line structures which progressively become solid shapes.

ABCDEFGHIJKL
XY abcdefghijklm

Traditional distortions
The alphabet (*above*) is one designed by 18th century Italian typesetters. This example is called Bodoni in which the verticals are maximized and the horizontals minimized.

Two way stretch
The alphabet (*right*) by the designer Edward Wright has its proportions stretched horizontally, but the verticals are minimized.

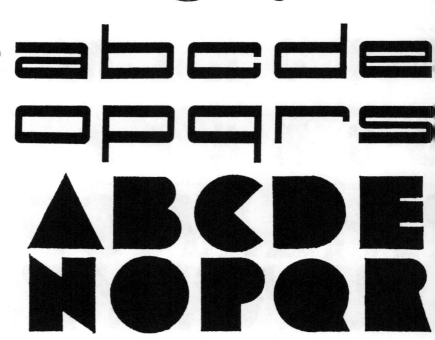

Solid letters
The French designer Jean Larcher has developed these 1970s letterforms to such an extent that they are barely recognizable. Each has perhaps the maximum weight distortion possible without losing its basic identifiable character.

Fill in

The letters A, B, C, V (*right*) are solid shapes. We only realize they are letters when we search for meaning. The panel of text (*far right*) mischievously challenges our reading abilities as the letters are rendered beyond recognition. The first word is JANNER (with a lower case a), the next word is SONNTAG (Sunday).

Task
Painting letters

Using a sheet of black paper, paint a row of letters in white without first pencilling in shapes. Imagine you are carving out the forms. Only add white to the spaces around the forms until they appear as letters.

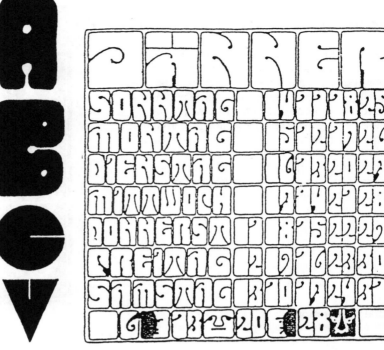

Decorating letters

In the production of books, before printing, the first letter of a page or paragraph was often enlarged or decorated. This letter, an initial, was usually drawn by an artist with a brush, whereas the text was produced by a scribe with a pen. These large letters became vehicles for imaginative experiments and fun. Later designers devised individual letters or alphabets intended for specific applications, deriving their inspiration from elements of fantasy, natural materials or just enthusiastic penmanship.

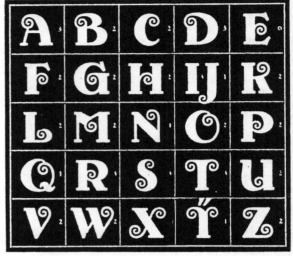

Simple embellishment
Basic letters (*above*) with a simple spiral added.

Added decoration
Three alphabets originally with traditional forms (upper one is 16th century Gothic, middle one classical Roman capitals, bottom one Italic) but now all decorated.

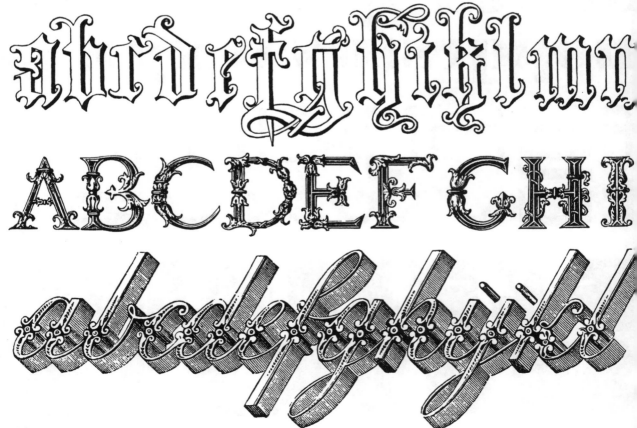

30

Living forms

The two letters (*left*) are versions adapted in the nineteenth century from medieval scribes' decorative initials. The letter (*right*) is by a designer who has gone wild with enthusiasm for his penmanship skills. This letter explodes like a released watch spring. It sings with energy.

Home made letters

The alphabets (*right*) are made as if of materials. These solutions are fun but hard to utilize when devising a word. The shapes need to be modified when combined.

Task
Cheese words

Using the examples (*below*) design the remainder of the alphabet in a similar style.

Task
Material forms

Choose any simple word and draw the letters as if made from some material like bricks, bones, or leaves.

Embellishing letters

Letters made of animals or humans (anamorphic forms) freeze the figures in contortions of their limbs and bodies. No real attention is paid to the anatomy, perspective or physically possible positions. Successful alphabets are those which retain their character recognition, but whose inventive distortions are startling and often humorous. Designers also enjoy taking traditional letterforms and adding other elements to create busy shapes and styles.

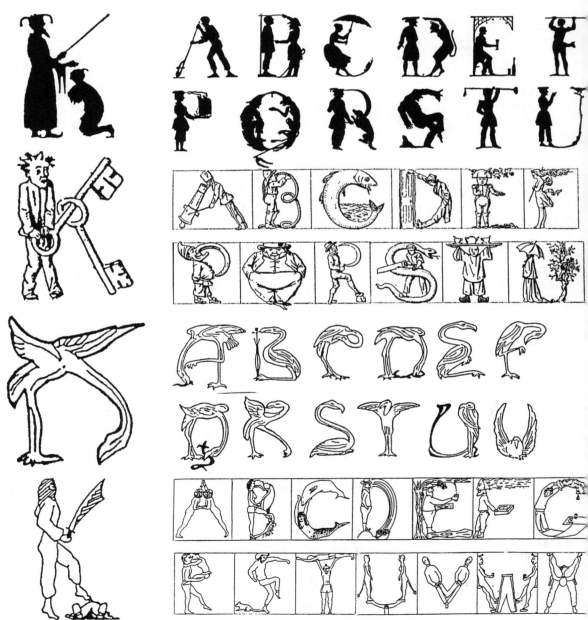

Task

Doodles
Sketches (*left*) are the first steps towards designing a crazy humanist alphabet. Try yourself to develop the other letters of the alphabet along these lines. Remember that invention is more fun than conformity.

Human letters
The alphabets (*below*) were probably intended as initial letters in 19th century magazines. The silhouette version has some unsuccessful letters, such as N U V W X Y and Z because the elements are not of a common thickness and the overall shape of the letter is obscure.

Bird letters
Nineteenth century initial letters formed from the contortions of a crane or cranes.

Contemporary letters
An alphabet designed by Brian (aged 16) as an exercise in imaginative composition.

© DIAGRAM

33

Alphabets as other cultures

Because we are so familiar with the basic forms of letters, designers can play games with the shapes to imply that the alphabets belong to their cultures. These "joke" solutions are mostly useful in advertising where the type of culture to be implied is helped by putting the message into the appropriate writing style.

Task
Ethnic alphabet
Search through magazines to find examples of an ethnic style and from the few letters construct your own alphabet.

1 abcdeff ghijklmnop

2 ABCDEFGHIJKLMNOP

3 ABCDEFGHIJKLMNOP

4 ABCDEFGH

PQRSTUVW

fghijklmnopqrst

34

Mimicry

The four alphabets (*below*) steal features from other language script styles to pretend to be derived from other cultures.

1 A script using the mannerisms of Sanskrit to purport to be an Indian alphabet.

2 A script exploiting the thicks and thins and the tails of the Hebrew alphabet.

3 Linear, angular forms of the ancient Greek pottery inscribers.

4 Broad and thin brush strokes characteristic of Chinese calligraphers.

5 Detail from an advertisement promoting a Japanese electrified heater where the designer not only emulates the brush style of oriental calligraphy but also places the characters in a vertical arrangement similar to Japanese literature.

qrstuvwxyz

QRSTUVWXYZ

QRSTUVWXYZ

JKLMNO

XYZ abcde

uvwxyz&!?

5

THE KOTATSU IS DESIGNED TO

HEAT THE PERSON, NOT THE ROOM

IT PROVIDES MAXIMUM EFFICIENCY

©DIAGRAM

Review

How can we judge a bad letter shape? Only experience can tell, and then only your personal reactions can be applied. Sophisticated forms are the cultural luxury that may be rejected by a designer in favor of naive and primitive forms more suitable to the design task. You can design your own letterforms and you can judge their relevance to the application.

Stretch
The Austrian designer, Alfred Roller, of a 1902 Vienna art exhibition poster (*left*) has picked out the letter S to link the word Secession with the bizarre letters below.

Historical styles
The rows of letters (*above*) are by 19th century designers except for the first row which is an adaptation of a medieval pen style called Black Letter (Gothic).

Task
Historical styles
Search magazines for examples of 19th century solutions. These are usually more elaborate than current styles. Cut out the discoveries and stick them in your scrapbook.

Form and function
The examples (*right*) show how far a designer can test our powers of recognition. We expect the letters to make words so we search for identification in the obscure inventions of designers. The third row is particulalry mischievous as at first glance it appears not to contain letters. These imaginative 1970s designs are by the French typographer Jean Larcher.

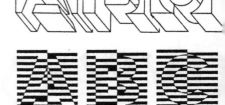

Current sources

Present-day dry transfer catalogs offer an enormous selection of bizarre styles. The manufacturers have commissioned designers to create alphabets for every conceivable need. These wonderful sources of alphabet designs can be used as the starting point of a new idea. See examples (*right*).

Task
Dry transfer
Order dry transfer letter catalogs. Do not copy the letters, study their design solutions as inspiration for your own.

Task
Mimicry
Design your own alphabet for a culture you like, maybe Viking, Aztec, American, Indian or Russian.

Task
Past sources
Where available, printers' catalogs can also provide you with ideas. Those of the 19th century often contain widely distorted alphabets intended for display and heading use. The larger alphabets were carved in wood and mounted alongside the lead characters of normal type.

Task
Rare sources
It is now extremely difficult to obtain what was once a very popular source of alphabet solutions: books on penmanship. These had examples by writing masters who, wishing to show their dexterity, would include wild swirling letters. Visit your local library and ask if they have any old calligraphy books.

Chapter 2

Ethnic differences

The examples of newspapers from around the world (*below*) contain different methods of formulating words. Each uses different alphabet systems and, in the case of oriental publications, individual characters for the words. Nevertheless it can easily be seen that the emphasis on the important words is achieved by size, weight and position. The levels of the message are evaluated and expressed similarly in each newspaper.

WORDS

The style by which you dress the words, your choice of letterforms and type style, produce a tone of voice. The word could shout, whisper, implore, command, instruct, suggest, or imply, all by the style chosen to produce the characters. In newspapers this range is used to organize the order in which we read the information. Key facts are placed in a prominent position and are usually larger and in bold. In the urban environment the words become a visual noise around us, calling to our attention services or instructions. Word styles are very often the result of cultural mannerisms learnt from drawing the letters. A Dutchman, Spaniard and a Pole would all draw the alphabet slightly differently having learnt to form the shapes at school and under the influence of distinct cultural heritages.

The meaniug of words

Words are groups of letters arranged to convey a meaning. The letters individually or collectively indicate sounds. Each group of letters produces an impression of horizontal spiky shapes which resemble marching rows of insects. It is the shape of the word which we read and not the individual letters. A mistake within a word is instantly recognizable to an experienced reader because the pattern does not match a mental picture they have of the word. An unconscious memory of the shapes is superimposed over each word to fit. Experienced raeders will have noticed that the title of this page has a word in which one of the letters is upside down and that this sentence contians two words with the letters in the wrong order.

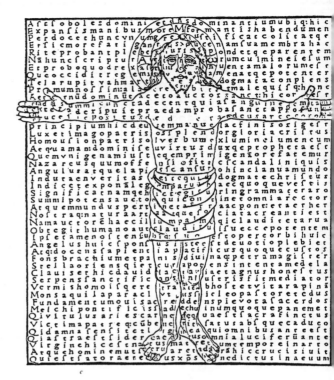

Word structure
This group of 25 letters (*left*) from the Forum in Rome has been arranged so that the reader can read the same Latin words horizontally and vertically. They have the added magic of being able to be read forward, backward, downward or upward.

Picture words
Words can be substituted by picture words or abbreviations. In 1975 the designer Milton Glaser used a heart (*below left*) to represent the word "love" and the customary initials NY to represent New York. The message reads I LOVE NEW YORK.

Directional reading
We normally read words horizontally from left to right. The words TUO YAW (*right*) appear on a window which from the other side read WAY OUT.

Intervals
The rows of letters in this 9th century Carolingian manuscript (*above*) have little meaning even to a reader of Latin. This is because the scribe has written the text as a continuous line of letters without regard for gaps between words.

Word gaps
Because the groups of letters make words, the arrangement into words of a number of letters depends upon the spaces between the letters. The two words NOSMO KING (*below*) appear on the two sides of windows and in English read NO SMOKING. The gap was caused by a window support.

S A T O R
A R E P O
T E N E T
O P E R A
R O T A S

TUO

NOSMO

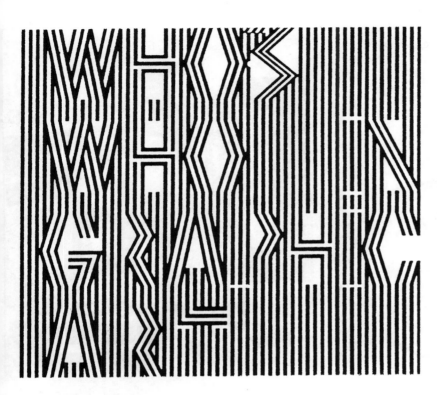

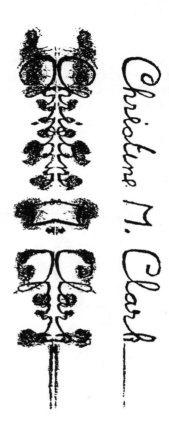

Background noise
Just as one voice talking in a crowded room is hard to hear, so words mixed among busy backgrounds cause us to strain to identify them. The designer of this book jacket (*above*), F M Nedo, has hidden the title WHO'S WHO IN GRAPHIC ART in a buzz of lines. Legibility must be the prime concern when we wish to convey information. Unreadable text means the message is missed.

Hidden origins
Groups of letters can become words when originally they represented more complex statements. The composer Verdi's name (*below right*) has the initials of the words Vittorio Emmanuele Re D'Italia. The Swedish company ESSELTE (*below*) was originally called Sveriges Litografiska Tyrckerier, whose initials, SLT, are pronounced in Europe as Esselte. The petroleum company Standard Oil is known world wide as ESSO.

Creatures
The pattern (*above*) was produced by writing the name *Christine M Clark* in pen and ink, and before the ink was dry folding the paper along the base of the word to produce a blotted mirror image of the word.

YAW ESSELTE

KING

Verdi

ESSO

The shape of words

Designers can break the rules of word formations by rearranging the units while still retaining the message. The more familiar we are with the word the easier it is to distort and still retain its identity.

Canto primo.

MIGLIOR acqua alza le vele
omai la navicella del mio ingegno,
che lascia dietro a sè mar sì crudele.
E canterò di quel secondo regno,
ove l'umano spirito si purga,

Letter patterns
The detail (*above left*) in a Dante poem has an introductory statement where the designer Anna Simons has worked Dante's words PER CORRER into a structure of letters by having various sizes of letter. Popular words easily identified, such as the French aperitif Dubonnet, afford the designer in the example (*above right*) the chance to jumble the letters but retain the message.

Overall shapes
Each word has its own unique shape and the grouping can produce other shapes if the designer selects combinations of capitals and lower case. The word Prague has three basic forms, each offering obstacles or possibilities for exploitation.

No shape
The word FORD in capitals is a solid rectangle shape. The designer of this 1956 poster (*right*), Herbert Leupin of Basle, has placed the modular letters vertically but not aligned under one another.

Inventive thinking
The Parisian designer Michel Leiris has had the brilliant idea of writing the word AMOUR so that each subsequent letter is within the preceding one. This is truly breaking new ground.

Breaking the mold
Each letter's basic form requires the designer to retain its elements. Words that are easily identified can have letters distorted beyond individual recognition. The letter F (*below*) is unrecognizable but at the beginning of the word FINAND it fits easily.

Constructionism
Designers frequently modify all the letters to comply with their overall design style. In the example (*below*) the word STEINER has no curves, the S and R are constructed from straight elements. The word JUGEND (*below*), used on an 1896 magazine cover, has been transformed by the designer Reimerschmid into entwining curves.

| Karl Steiner | Bauschreinerei und Möbelfabrik Laden- und Schaufensterausbau Coiffeureinrichtungen | Zürich 11/50 Hagenholzstra Telefon 46 43 |

©DIAGRAM

Energizing words

Words are an assembly of letters which are usually all the same size, weight and character. Varying the size of individual letters within words and from one word to another can have a dramatic effect on their overall appearance. Designers call attention to features of words by varying these elements to heighten the dramatic effect of the words.

Is our ARMY in Kharki now dressed

L cuchillo para templar l
de fer qual lo pinto el Pal
tado, que tenga buen azer
do, de buen talle y de buen
bo quiere fer groffezuelo, y quadra
brando conel no fe vaya dela mano:
que el corte mas, y menos fegu el tam

First letters
In the children's A B C book of c1900 (*above*) the first letter of each sentence (the sequential letters of the alphabet) is enlarged. The word associated with the letter is presented in capitals so that the young reader may link the introductory letter to the individual word.

Initial letters
Before the invention of printing, books were produced by a scribe writing out every letter and word. These hand-drawn books very often had two different craftsmen working on the page at different times. A scribe would write the text (using a quill or reed pen) but would leave a space for the first letter of the first word. This space would then be filled in by another scribe (usually using a brush) who drew out an enlarged letter that was often highly decorated. Detail (*above left*) is from a 16th century hand-written Latin religious Book of Hours. The example (*center left*) is from a Spanish 17th century printed book in which the printer has inserted large carved initial letters to imitate the earlier calligraphic style.

Varying the size of letters
Modern designers can behave misleadingly, knowing that the reader expects the shapes to make letters and the letters to make words. They often jumble up the basic principles of lettering and calligraphy to produce memorable and exciting designs. This technique only works when you wish to excite and interest the reader. It is less suitable when you are trying to inform the reader or assist understanding. The name of the pop group (*left*) has its letter sizes mixed and lower case letters are inserted among the capitals.

No-rules style

Having disregarded the principle of having all the letters the same size, style and weight in a word, the designer can even replace letters such as the r in this example (*right*) with a bent line.

Size and emphasis

The 19th century poster (*right*) uses differing sizes for each line of text. By putting the more important parts in a larger typeface the basic message of the continuous text is broken up and key words attract the attention of the reader. As the lines are often made from capital letters (which unify the word shapes) the designer has selected a variety of styles to further increase the interest and produce patterns of emphasis.

Energizing words

Normally, all the letters in a word are the same size. However, designers often diminish the size of the letters towards the end of the word to give it a sense of dynamism. The example (*above*) is from the label of a box of fireworks, where the receding letters and the scratchy forms give energy to the design.

RODNEY BOD

1869. **May 10th.** 1869.

GREAT EVENT

Rail Road from the Atlantic to the Pacific

GRAND OPENING
— OF THE —
PASSENGER TRAINS LEAVE

OMAHA

ON THE ARRIVAL OF TRAINS FROM THE EAST.

THROUGH TO SAN FRANCISCO

In less than Four Days, avoiding the Dangers of the Sea!

Travelers for Pleasure, Health or Business

Will find a Trip over The Rocky Mountains Healthy and Pleasant.

LUXURIOUS CARS & EATING HOUSES

ON THE UNION PACIFIC RAIL ROAD.

PULLMAN'S PALACE SLEEPING CARS

RUN WITH ALL THROUGH PASSENGER TRAINS.

GOLD, SILVER AND OTHER MINERS!

Now is the time to seek your Fortunes in Nebraska, Wyoming, Arizona, Washington, Dakotah Colorado, Utah, Oregon, Montana, New Mexico, Idaho, Nevada or California.

CONNECTIONS MADE AT

CHEYENNE for DENVER, CENTRAL CITY & SANTA FE

AT OGDEN AND CORINNE FOR HELENA BOISE CITY, VIRGINIA CITY, SALT LAKE CITY AND ARIZONA

THROUGH TICKETS FOR SALE AT ALL PRINCIPAL RAILROAD OFFICES!

Be Sure they Read via Platte Valley or Omaha

Company's Office 72 La Salle St., opposite City Hall and Court House Square, Chicago.
CHARLES E. NICHOLS, Ticket Agent.

G. P. GILMAN.   JOHN P. HART.   J. BUDD.   W. SNYDER.

Words in boxes

Words usually appear as a rectangular block of text in which the lines are horizontal and read from left to right. The cumulative effect of this block of text is like a texture. When a word appears in isolation the spatial tension is heightened. Designers often work out their ideas in miniature so that they can judge the overall effect of the way they have arranged the words.

Pattern-making
The sketches (*above*) are for a greetings card design containing a poem. The designer has scribbled simple design roughs to depict possible arrangements of the words.

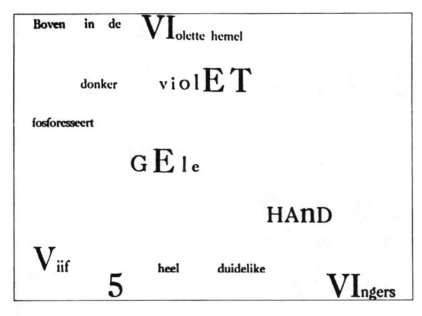

Task
Judging patterns
Pin one of your designs to the wall of your room. Position yourself as far away as you can and sketch the basic arrangements of the elements. The same effects can be achieved by obtaining a greatly reduced photocopy of one of your designs.

Spatial tensions
The Dutch designer Van Ostaijen used the open space of the rectangle (*above*) to suspend the individual words in a tension of space. This style of word play was a particular favorite of the artists working in the Dadaist style during the 1920s.

Angular tensions
Horizontal is not necessarily the best, as the poster (*right*) shows. The designer has enlarged the main text and tilted it so that it appears to be going beyond the available space.

Task
Directional reading
Make a collection of examples of words reading in various directions. Although these are not all in everyday use, you may find that the vertical designs are often used on signs in inner cities, particularly on cafes and bars.

Stepped designs
The Berlin city bear climbing the word is from a German matchbox cover (*above*). Package designs often contain examples where the designer has played with the arrangements to obtain interesting combinations of shapes.

Wavy designs
Only three of the 10 lines of words on this 19th century label are horizontal. Most of them twist and curve to form interlocking patterns which resemble ribbons (*above right*).

Task
Wavy
Carefully trace a word containing over 10 letters along a horizontal line. Then draw a curved line, either a wavy one or one which forms part of a circle. Trace the word again using this curved line. Take care to adjust the letter spacing to maintain the unified appearance of the letters forming a single word.

Directional reading
The six boxes (*right*) contain the same word arranged in a variety of ways:
1 Forward, reading horizontally
2 Backward, reading horizontally
3 Forward, reading diagonally downward
4 Backward, reading diagonally upward
5 Vertical, reading downward
6 Vertical, reading upward

ANCHOVY PASTE
For SANDWICHES &c.
BY APPOINTMENT
PURVEYORS to HerMAJESTY
PREPARED BY
CROSSE & BLACKWELL
ESTABLISHED IN 1706
21 SOHO SQUARE
LONDON

1 MOSCOW

2 WOCSOM

3 MOSCOW

4 WOCSOM

5 MOSCOW

6 WOCSOM

Words as texture

Just as each individual brick in a wall loses its identity when viewed from a distance, each word, when seen against a background of all the surrounding words becomes part of the visual texture of a statement. Traditionally, in print, words are dark marks on a light background and their textural appearance is a result of the style of lettering and the scale of the words.

Textural words
The 16th century Bible title page (*above*) contains both printed Latin text and handwritten German notes (by Luther in 1542/3). This example, which is greatly reduced, shows the almost knitted quality of the handwritten parts.

Spatial textures
The decorative embellishments in the Dutch announcement (*above right*) link the words and help to give a tonal quality to the individual lines.

Imaginative textures
The American designer John Berg produced this extremely inventive design (*top*) in which the letters of the word "Chicago" blend with the patterns and whirls of a thumb print. Ideas like this can appear to be obvious when they are presented, but are, in fact, the unique inventions of a fresh mind.

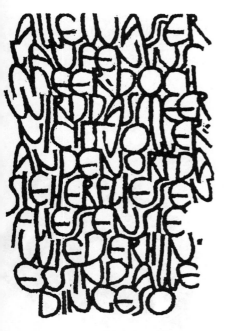

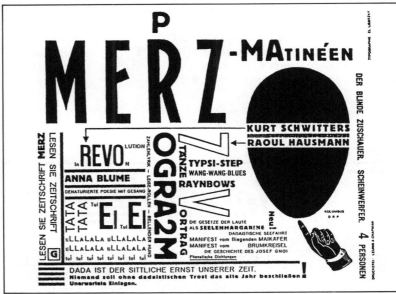

Structured texture

The German designer Hans-Joachim Burgert has linked each line of text (*above left*) with each row of letters to produce a structure which is difficult to read (even for a German!). It can only be interpreted using the knowledge which the reader already has. This technique is not intended to convey information. The designer has simply used the letters as a starting-point when building a pattern.

Monumental pattern

Classical buildings in Greece and Rome often incorporated textural statements. These Greek patterns of letters (*left*) could be read because the reader was often familiar with the word structures and so could separate out the words without needing spaces between them to aid their understanding.

Variable textures

The typographical designers of the 1920s often mixed sizes, weights and positions to produce textures in their pattern-making. Observe how the designer in the example (*above*) has used two sizes of letter for the word REVOlution.

Task

Pattern-making

Write out in capital letters a short quotation or poem. Eliminate the line spaces so that each line butts up to the line above it. Make each letter occupy the same width as its neighbors. This is made easier if you work on tracing paper over a sheet of graph paper or a square grid. The resulting lattice work may be unintelligible at first sight but it helps you to see the pattern of the letterforms.

Accidental patterns

The Italian telegram message (*left*) was intended to be read. Its decorative quality is the result of the line-feed mechanism in the tranmission machine operating in such a way that each letter stands directly below the one above it.

```
IL "KOLO" FRA LE MANIFESTAZIO
NI ESTERIORI PIU' AFFASCINANTI
DEL COSTUME JUGOSLAVO E' SEN-
Z'ALTRO DA PORRE LA LUNGA TEO
RIA DEI BALLI NAZIONALI, CHE
SI DIFFERENZIANO NOTEVOLMENTE
FRA LORO A SECONDA DELLE REGIO
NI IN CUI SONO DIFFUSI.
IL "KOLO" E' UNO DI QUESTI E
FRA I PIU' DIFFUSI. SI RIALLAC
CIA, QUESTO BALLO POPOLARE SER
BO, ALLA ANTICA TRADIZIONE
DEI BALLI FOLKLORISTICI SLAVI
ED UCRAINI.
ECCO UNO STUDIO DI DETTO BALLO
IN UNA SERIE DI FIGURE OBBLI
GATE ESEGUITE DAL COMPLESSO
DEL TEATRO DI STATO DI BELGRADO
```

Review

By grouping the individual letters into established combinations, words are formed. These of course vary depending on the language so that the 42 characters available can make an almost infinite range of individual words. When we learn to read we quickly lose the need to memorize the combinations of letters, and develop the ability to identify words by their overall shape. This enables designers to test our interpretations by producing words copied from hundreds of different lettering styles.

Texture

Large quantities of words in typographical presentations are normally grouped into blocks. These groupings create the illusion of changing textural surfaces. The Dutch magazine design (*above*) contains a window of white space into which a larger word has been inserted. Designers who use this technique often consider their work to be similar to that of an architect designing a facade. The text complies with an inner structure, a grid, on which the designer positions all the elements so that they interrelate.

Noisy words

This early Soviet poster (*above right*) uses size to indicate the intended volume and importance of the political message. It is often very helpful when working out a design to simply imagine that weight and size are equal to the impact of the words. Big words are easier to read and so appear to be more important.

Task
Texture
Select a design containing a great deal of text and make a reduced-down photocopy of it. The smaller your photocopy, the less legible the words become. The overall texture of the design becomes the clearest feature.

MŪSJK JM Lēben dēr VÖLKER AM 21. JŪLJ 20 Ūhr dJRJGJERT JM ŌPERNhAUS FJTelbeRG WARSₐhAUS beRÜhMTER dJRJGENT WERKE POLNJ5ₐhER MEJSTER

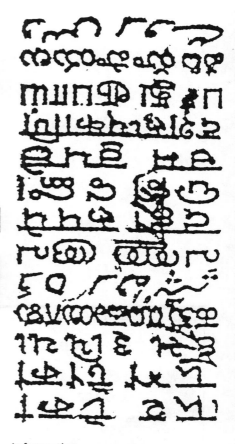

Criss-cross
The Italian Studio Boggeri has used the possibilities of creating spatial tensions by placing Total gasoline slogans of 1940 in a square (*left*). The text is all in capitals and only two sizes are used, but the interest is achieved by having to read interlocking lines at right angles to one another.

Anything goes!
The 1927 phonetic type design (*above*) is by Dutchman Kurt Schwitters. Because the readers can be assumed to follow the message, the words have been distorted by the insertion of characters from both the capital and the lower case alphabets. In the case of the word "July" the letters have been twisted to satisfy the designer's overall ambition of involving the reader in the deciphering of the message.

Information
The lines of text (*above*) are an enlarged detail from an Indian 10-rupee note. Each line says the same thing but is in one of the many different languages of India. Designers enjoy playing with the textural qualities of words but they also have a responsibility to maintain the message-carrying quality of the letter combinations.

Task
Spatial tension
You can create a sense of tension in your design using a cut-out rectangular hole. By moving this frame around your design you will find that you have many dynamic solutions. Whatever solution you create it is important to make the message always readable.

Chapter 3

When designing with words you should think about the overall effects of the words within the frame of your composition, and think of the words as possibly having individual features, as if they were depictions of objects or ideas. As we judge the total design by the spaces around the words as well as by the words' shapes, you should plan your design by making small sketches so that you can evaluate all of the elements at the same time.

Two-dimensional space
The American designer Robert Gage uses the words placed around the figure (*left*) to produce pauses and groupings in the sentence which hold the attention of the reader on this 1957 New York department store advertisement.

Three-dimensional space
The designer Josep Renau has substituted airplanes for the letter "V" in this 1937 Spanish Republican Civil War poster (*below*). The two arms of the "V" reach into space.

PICTURES

With some words you may be able to develop the three-dimensional qualities as if they receded or protruded or were solid forms. Occasionally you may even be able to make the words form a picture or pattern which may be only a slight distortion of their shapes.

Words express ideas and these ideas can be illustrated by imaginative adaptations of letterforms or by trying to depict the idea in the way the word is displayed. The letter styles have characters which can be used to enhance the meaning of the words, so you should choose a style which you think suits the word's character.

Words and letters were originally developed from pictures, and designers often try to establish a pictorial quality for words. This is often achieved by the arrangement of the initial letters to form an interrelated pattern. These solutions, called monograms or letter-logos, are ideally suited for use when establishing an identity. They become a badge or emblem, replacing the words describing a company or a person.

Emblems
The designer F H Ehmcke has used his initials to form the teeth of a key (*left*), for his own 1928 Munich exhibition. Many designers enjoy exploring the shapes of groups of letters, but this is a particularly clever combination.

Pictorial words
The name of the newspaper *Der Tag* (*left*) has been drawn as cascading water in this 1900 German advertisement. The designer Ludwig Sütterlin must have realized that the branching arms of the capital T are like a fountain's spray.

Ideas
The players in the Spanish ball game Jai Alai (similar to pelota) use a racket made from basket-work which is shaped like a scoop. The designer Bud Jarrin has used the capital J (*above*) to suggest this implement. He also wittily converts the dot of the lower case i to be the ball (pelota).

53

Composition

Horizontal lines of text can be arranged in relationship to one another and to the edges so that their sequential importance is enhanced. Working within a rectangular frame you can consider the effect of positioning each line knowing that you can rely on the reader having some understanding of your message.

1

JOHANN SEBASTIAN BACH

2

JOHANN SEBASTIAN BACH

3

JOHANN SEBASTIAN BACH

4

JOHANN SEBASTIAN BACH

Position
Rows of letters can be grouped horizontally in four ways(*above*):
1 Centered
Each line is centrally positioned directly underneath the one above it.
2 Justified
Each line has the letters or the word spacing stretched or compressed so that all the lines take up the same width.

3 Ranged (flush) left, ragged right
The first letter of each line is directly under the first letter of the line above it.
4 Ranged (flush) right, ragged left
The last letter of each line is directly under the last letter of the line above.

1

CLICK CLACK CLUCK

2

CLICK CLACK CLUCK

3

CLICK CLACK CLUCK

One size

The movie poster (*above*) uses only one size, weight, character and color. The designer achieves his effects by the skillful positioning. The tension comes from the other elements of the composition such as the city lights.

Two sizes

The 1955 Swiss electoral committee poster (*right*) by Armin Hofmann uses two sizes, large for the word "ja" (*yes*) and a smaller one for the remaining text. The composition's power is achieved by the dominant element of black and the feeling that the reader peers into a narrow space in order to read the text.

All ways

The 19th century poster (*left*) uses as many different styles, sizes, capitals and lower case as the designer can get into the area. The rectangle is filled with the larger words increased in size until they fill up the available space.

Six ways

The words click, clack and cluck appear in three rows in the panels (*below*). The changes to the final words by the insertion of a different style letter is achieved by:

1 Position
Moving one of the normal letters to another position.

2 Size
Inserting a letter which is larger but in the same style.

3 Weight
Inserting a letter which is the same style but much heavier (bolder).

4 Color
Inserting a letter the same size, style and weight, but in a different color. (Shown as an outline.)

5 Character
Inserting a letter from a different typeface (lettering style).

6 Techniques
Changing the method by which the letters are made. The previous rows of letters were made using dry transfer lettering. The U was drawn with a pencil.

Stepping into space

Creating letters which appear to be within a spatial area can offer you very exciting possibilities. Simply to add a thickness to the forms, or to imagine the row of letters in the word to be bending, receding or moving in some interesting way into the space of your page, opens up the possibilities of creating arresting designs. This technique is only advisable for short statements and single words.

Solid forms
The three examples (*above*) are outline versions of basic letters. The student has applied a side section of solid black tone to indicate whether the forms reveal a top edge, side edge or part-top and side.

Overlap
(*Above left*) Individual letters can be overlapped, either to each of the adjacent letters or to duplicates of themselves.

Recession
(*Above*) Although our reason tells us that the smaller letters are on the same surface as the larger ones, the first impression gained is that the letters are all of the same size but are receding into the picture area. The artistic convention of creating the impression of depth by having larger objects in the foreground and smaller ones in the background is influencing our interpretation of this design.

Task
Solid forms
Trace a simple word from a magazine. Move your tracing down and to the left a little. Retrace the outlines of the letters without crossing any of the lines of the first tracing. You now have letterforms which have a three-dimensional appearance.

Absent forms
These alphabets (*above* and *right*) are not drawn. Their appearance is deduced from the sides of the supposedly solid shapes. This technique is particularly successful with single words which you wish to stand out from the surface of the page.

Solid forms

The letters can be drawn as if constructed from solid materials. The examples (*left*) are taken from dry transfer catalogs in which the designers have created the illusion of solid shapes by adding areas indicating shadow or volume.

Into space

In the South African World War II poster design (*right*) the artist has placed the lower text on the side of a box so that the letters are within the compositional space. The message entering the ballot box is drawn flat on the surface, but appears to be flying through space.

Curved space

The letters in the logotype (*right*) have been constructed to appear as if they were on a curved surface. Only the letters E and T (in the foreground) are correctly formed. The other letters are distorted so that they appear to be part of a curved group of solid letters.

Making pictures

You can exploit the pattern quality of words by considering them as total shapes, or as ribbons of shapes. You can run the lines of a text into a pattern that forms a picture. You can bend the outline shapes of the words to fit the areas representing objects. You can use the white spaces between each letter and word as a design motif. You can substitute letters with pictures or symbols, and you can combine the individual letters to make patterned structures.

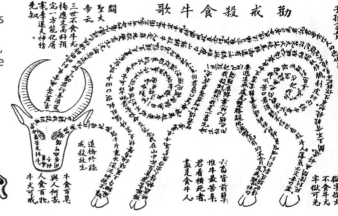

Ribbons
The American company emblem (*above*) uses the traditional heraldic device of placing the rows of letters along a band. This was a very popular technique in the 19th century, but now appears to us as fussy and too elaborate.

Task
Picture sources
Keep a scrapbook of examples cut from newspapers of designers playing games with letters and words. It is surprising how many examples you can find in daily newspaper advertisements.

Picture ribbons
The Chinese poster (*above*) of 1911 runs the lines of copy around to form the outline of a bull with prayers for the animal's protection. Traditionally, Chinese text could be read horizontally left to right or vertically top to bottom. The grass in this picture is the latter and the text above the bull the former.

Textural patterns
The German baroque poet J R Karst has designed his 1667 piece "Fern" in the shape of that plant. The letters inside represent the leaf's texture (*left*) and the key word has a double meaning. This technique of forming pictures with lines of copy can be irritating if the shapes created obscure the text message. The Italian Futurist poet Pino Masnata (*right*) has squeezed his 1918 words of passion into shapes representing a plate, knife, fork and food.

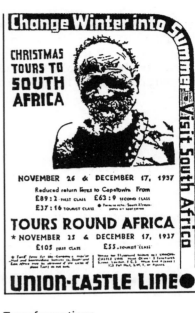

Reading spaces
The white spaces within the letters and between the words have been used by the Austrian designer Julius Klinger to hold together the elements of this Berlin spring art exhibition poster (*above*). We read the bands of words as if they were a dark fence of lines seen against a bright background.

Picture elements
The need of companies to establish a distinguishable and memorable identity with the word describing them has led designers to produce word shapes that often have image substitutions for letters, distorted letters, or pictorial elements added. The five modern examples (*below*) are a selection of typical company emblems.

Transformations
The travel poster (*above*) has a line of copy which begins as white on a dark background. Not only does it turn a corner and descend an edge of the design, but it also becomes black on white.

Task
Seeing words as shapes
Copy a simple word from a magazine by placing the original upside down under your tracing paper. You will more likely see the shapes when you are not reading the word. A similar task would be to trace a word from a language you cannot read.

Forming circles

Because we read the word or words in a statement as a continuous ribbon of marks, designers can bend the row of characters into any shape they choose, as long as they retain their legibility. All the designs on these two pages are examples of lettering having been arranged to fit within a circle.

A1

A2

Lettering arrangements
The message within the circle can be arranged in four different ways.
A The words are horizontal and arranged so that they fit within the area.
B The words are arranged around bands within the circle, either all running in the same direction or in either direction.
C The words are one continuous band spiralling into or out of the center.
D The words are distorted to appear as if on the surface of a sphere.

A1 The name DUVAL JANVIER in which both words share the common central letter V.

A2 REKLAMA MECHANO (type composition by Henryk Berlewi, Warsaw c1925) in which the letters at the sides are reduced to fit within the circle of this advertising agency's trademark.

A3 Russian rouble coin for centenary of Napoleon's defeat in which the letters are centered in rows.

A4 A German 1962 type design by Hans-Joachim Burgert.

B1 British 19th century cold cream circular jar lid.

B2 Postal franking stamp, France 1957, continuing both horizontal and circular techniques.

B3 Brand name on a New York powder jar seal, lettering by Tommy Thompson c1937.

B4 A cheese box label, France c1930.

A3

A4

B1

B2

B3

B5 The calligrapher Irene Sutton's journal of a 1934 English holiday.

C Early 18th century German writing master I C Hittensperger's demonstration of spiral skills celebrates God's wisdom.

D The original company logo for IBM c1945.

Task
Proverb
Write a short proverb inside a circle.

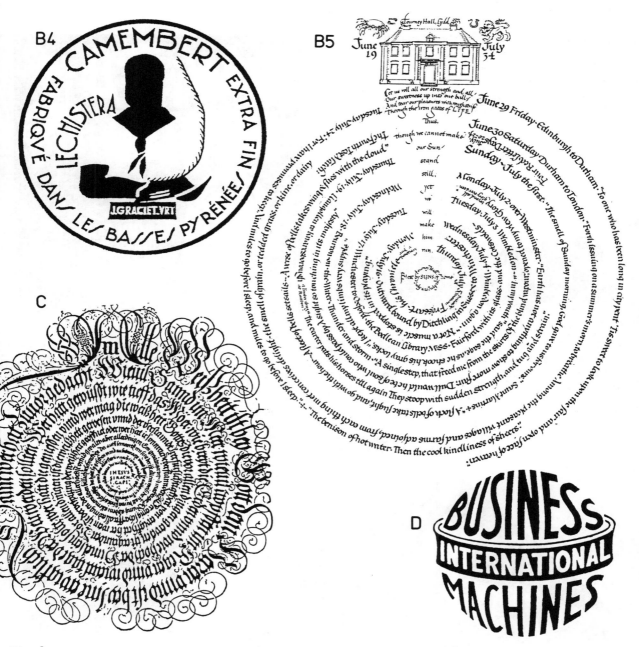

Task
Circular prose
The aim is to find the correct sized circle for a continuous ring of text around the circumference. Draw a series of circles from the same center point but with radii at ½in (12.5mm) intervals. Begin a short line of prose, perhaps your full name or a proverb, writing it around the circumference of one of the circles. Should your solution not extend all the way round, repeat the text in a circle closer to the center point. If your text exceeds the available ring space, repeat on a circle farther from the center.

Task
Word shapes
Copy a series of words in a language you do not know; you could find a short poem in a library book in an unfamiliar foreign language. Because you cannot "read" the text you are more able to direct your attention toward the shapes of the letters and words.

Expressing ideas

Words convey ideas, and the choice of letterforms can help. Both the selection of a style and the method by which it is drawn can in some way indicate the character of the subject. Because letter styles are the clothes words wear, you can dress your message in any style you think appropriate.

Slogans
The word SOLIDARNOSC (Solidarity) has since 1981 become a representation of Polish political dissent. The written style of this slogan (*above*) is made to look like a marching column of protesting workers with the Polish flag.

Task
Mood
Choose a word that describes a mood and then select a letterform to express it. Perhaps the word is Depressed, Jolly, Angry or Dizzy. Try your idea on dark paper, or use colored inks, or collage (cut out from newsprint).

Capturing mood
Designers of movie posters and book jackets often need to convey the mood of a subject by both images and words. The design (*above*) has the main title's letters quivering with fear.

quinquina

quin

quina

© DIAGRAM

62

baile de máscaras
del Circulo de bellas
Artes
1928

Expressive lines
The Spanish poster (*above*) has lines of text "dancing" under the feet of the figures. By arranging the letters in a wobbly row a festive feeling is conveyed with the information.

Expressive letters
The examples (*right*) by students explore the ability of letterforms to depict character. Although all the examples are of the same word, BERLIN, the way in which they are drawn suggests many different interpretations of the word.

Establishing style
The persistent use of a very distinguishable letter style and colors over many years has enabled recent designers to convey the message even though the lettering is unreadable. The original 1939 calligraphic style of the French designer Charles Loupot (*far left*) has been transformed in a 1950s poster (*left*) where the word is mutilated but the message is still clear to those familiar with the aperitif company's graphic styling.

Making patterns

For individual letters representing words, the initials are often intertwined to form a single design element. These emblems, variously called monograms, logos, trade marks or marques (for automobile makes), are then used as symbolic but often enduring and more powerful representations of the spelled out words. Sizes, thicknesses and shapes are modified to form a single integrated unit, and, when successful, the design becomes more than the sum of its parts.

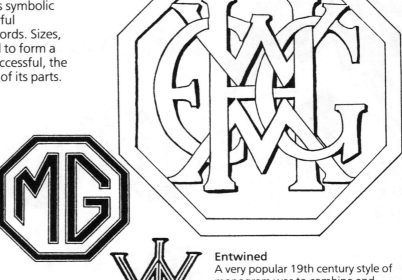

Distortion
The initials MG (meaning Morris Garages) (*right*) have been distorted to fit into an octagonal shape. The normally symmetrical M is twisted and the normally curved G is made of straight lines.

Combination
Letters can be superimposed either sharing common elements like the HB (1957 logo by Paul Rand for US publisher Harcourt Brace & Co) or simply overlapped like the WI (*right*), actually the signet of the Austrian goldsmith Wenzel Jamnitzer (1508-1588).

Framing
The outer limits of the letters can be used to form a frame that links and holds the letter in a trellis of shapes. The calligraphic lower case tb (*right*) sit in a strong almost square frame.

Shared parts
The row (*below*) is a student's experiment at combining the capital letters in the alphabet and then repeating the sequence combining upper and lower cases.

Entwined
A very popular 19th century style of monogram was to combine and intertwine the letters. This can develop into a visual puzzle where you have to establish how many letters are in the group. The monogram (*above*) contains E H G W M cut in stone by A J J Ayres for a pre-1937 garden path.

Task
Shared parts
Select any letter of the alphabet and explore ways in which it can be linked to all the other letters. Use a thick felt tip pen so that you are making strong bold shapes and not thin lines.

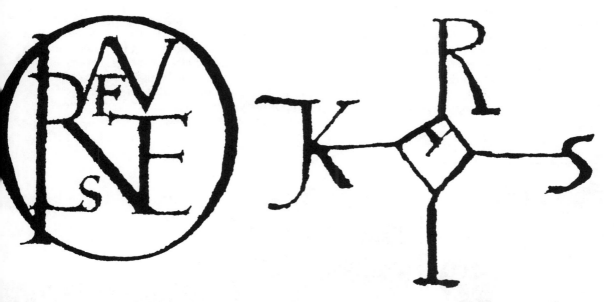

Monograms

There is an ancient tradition among craftsmen to sign their work not with a signature but with a device containing their initials or letters and shapes related to their profession. They were used by stone masons, carpenters, painters, gold and silversmiths, potters and calligraphers to identify their work. The design (*above*) is the monogram of the Early Christian scribe Furius Dionysius Filocalus, later calligrapher to Pope St Damasus I (366-383). Filocalus has very ably combined letters of differing sizes and used common elements to join them.

Seals

The pen-drawn monogram (*above*) was used by the great European Emperor Charlemagne (768-814) from the Latin for his name — KAROLUS. Kings, governments, churches and authorities have all used such stylized letters to represent their power. The badge or mark comes to represent the idea that the object on which it appears has the seal of approval or belongs to that authority, as in the "Bob on the Square Ranch" cattle brand, Texas 1875 (*right*).

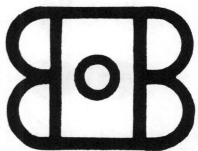

Task
Monograms
Begin to keep a source book of company emblems, symbols made from combining letters. They often appear in trade journals and newspaper advertisements.

Review

This chapter has been about the way that letters, when combined into words, create their own personalities. Lower case words are like insects, each with individual groups of protuberances above and below the central areas (ascenders and descenders). The rows of words in a sentence march across the page to form horizontal strands of shapes, each similar but in unique ways different.

Words are the visual noise in our environment. Wherever we go they are used either to inform, invite, warn or seduce us. In their printed form they call our attention to the subject they are describing by their selection of types and sizes. Letters are of course flat but they can be used as solid objects or to indicate receding space; or, most importantly, they can be used to convey ideas about the subject depicted.

Composition
The edges of the area containing the message act as a frame to which the elements relate. In addition, each of the separate elements relates to one another. The design (*above*) uses normally very small features to create an arresting impression. By greatly enlarging the punctuation to dwarf the letters, the designer has created a sense of crowdedness within the small area.

Task
Composition
Draw four 6in × 6in (150mm × 150mm) squares. Within each place a word. The first should shout, the second whisper, the third be as large as possible without being illegible, and the fourth should be surrounded in a sea of other words and become lost.

Space
Letters are of course flat shapes usually appearing on flat surfaces. Designers enjoy deceiving the eye by providing the illusion of solid or overlapping forms. The German trade show poster (*above*) by the designer Heinrich Joost links the letters D and G to suggest they are overlapping one another.

Task
Space
Draw a simple word so that its letters appear to be overlapping.

Pictures
Very often designers producing a company logo or emblem use the letters to create an image connected with the subject. The word cotton (*above*) has been developed by Walter Landor Associates for Cotton Inc (US 1973) so that the central pair of ts has become the stem of a cotton plant.

Task
Pictures
Select a simple word that suggests an image and develop the letterforms to portray the subject. For example try BALL, BUSH, HAND, SKULL, PEN, WINDOW or BOOK.

ХУДОЖЕСТВЕНЫЯ СОКРОВИЩА РОССІИ

Foreign words (*above*)

Letters in an unfamiliar language more clearly appear as an arrangement of shapes. This design by the Russian Ivan Bilibin was for the title page of the 1903 magazine *Art Treasures of Russia*. It uses characters from the Cyrillic alphabet and fills in the spaces with small blocks to achieve an overall patterned effect.

calder

```
sandy calder
ein mann wie ein baer
haar weiss-shirt rot helle hosen
alles rund nase mund und koerper
die warmherzige natur der humor
aus dem mundwinkel
fallen
    kurze
        eckige saetze
    aus groben fingern
    fliesst leichte bewegung
    des material
    stahldraht blech
    und gleichgewicht
    feine aeste mit
    grossen herbstblaettern
                gelbe
        schwarze  rote
                weisse
    balancierend im luftzug
    helle wolken
    beschreiben oben
    froh und farbig sich windend
    figuren ohne anfang und ende
    oder
    es wachsen
    dunkele riesige
    bodenstaendige gestalten
    signale kohlenhaendler spinnen
langse nase  schwarze witwe  schwarzes biest
hund  schuh  kaktus  die guillotine fuer acht

alexander calder hat in den fruehen dreissiger jahren
als erster amerikaner einen beitrag geliefert zur entwicklung
der bildenden kuenste: bewegung und gleichgewicht ohne maschine
sein lebenswerk gehoert geschichte und gegenwart
```

Patterns

The arrangement of much text within a rectangle creates patterns of horizontal lines which seen as areas of texture form patterns. The Dutch designer Willem Sandberg has taken the imaginative idea of setting his 1962 tribute to the American sculptor Alexander Calder into lines not vertically beneath one another, but set at an angle to form streams of prose.

Task
Patterns

Write out a short poem so that the lines run continuously but all the text occupies a diamond, circle or heart shape.

KING'S CROSS

Ideas

Words convey ideas, and designers make use of familiar ones. The London KING'S CROSS Railway Station has 10 letters in its name, but this designer has used an X and a crown to deliver the same message.

Task
Ideas

Devise a distorted arrangement of the letters in a word to convey its meaning. You could try JUMPED, CRAWL, SCRAMBLE, MIX-UP, or SQUASHED.

Emblem

This monogram signature is by the French painter Toulouse-Lautrec, Paris 1892. The Impressionist painters were often influenced by the recently imported Japanese crafts, the prints, vases and lacquered work of which carried devices designed by the craftsmen.

Task
Emblems

Using your initials, try a variety of ways of combining them in a circle. Then try a square and a diamond. Remember you can vary the size of each letter, or have them share common parts.

Chapter 4

Task
Energetic lines
Copy a line of curving forms of a word very carefully, then repeat the word over and over again. Work faster and faster until the word loses its inhibitions and becomes an energetic free expression of marks.

Task
Free expression
Draw a simple word using brush and paint, by the normal method of resting your hand on the surface while working. Repeat the same task but without your hand touching the paper for guidance. You will see how the second version is freer than the first.

The marks on a surface are the result of the method by which they were produced. Before printing and photography, each mark was the evidence of the method by which it was made. Present day processes enable the designer to use words which may have been produced by a wide variety of techniques. These are subsequently presented by reproduction. Beginners studying lettering design are often confused by the techniques of origination as these are further disguised by not revealing the size of the original artwork. It

Uninitiated
The simple signs displayed by retail stores often have a wonderful naive style which you can copy in your work. The innocence of joining up the letters on this sign (*above*) is an idea often applied to much more advanced works. If the design requires it, hand drawn forms need not be rejected in favor of more sophisticated solutions.

Traditional sources
Calligraphy examples in design history books (detail *top*), typography of earlier periods, and mannerisms of old styles can all be exploited in exploring new techniques. Although you cannot easily acquire the skills of master calligraphers, you can adopt their forms for your own use.

Deliberate accidents
The word (*above*) was drawn in slowly drying ink and while still wet was blown at through a straw. The close focused blasts of air blew dribbling streams of ink away from the main lines of the letters to produce this irregular yet strangely natural and organic solution.

METHODS

may have been drawn, the traditional calligraphic method. It may comprise dry transfer letters assembled individually. It may be typeset or photoset and recently may be produced by laser printers from computer letterform resources. Before beginning any task consider a number of factors which influence the resulting work. First, what tools are available? Although this may seem obvious, it is worth considering chalks, felt tip pens, or compass construction techniques. Second, what experience do you have of the tools?

One serious obstacle in the execution of a task is the difficulties met in mastering the tools. Third, what use is the task being put to? Will it be on permanent display? Is it for reproduction by photographic techniques? Can you draw it larger for reduction? Is it being created mechanically by typesetting or stencil?

This form of design often uses handcut letterforms which can be an inspiration as their irregularity disguises your inability to draw accurately correct letterforms.

Task
Techniques
Examine the alphabets in this book and try to deduce the method by which they were produced.

Graphic reproduction
This 1928 Campari poster was produced by a method called silkscreen printing, where the shapes are cut from a mask and the ink is squeezed through a fine mesh of silk onto the surface.

Exploration
Detail (*above*) of a design for use on a book jacket. It was made by scratching the forms into a tray of sand, then photographing the resulting shadowed forms. This free style can be arresting as the current profusion of letterforms can leave us bored and tired of similar methods of presentation. Try to explore new methods of making the letters and always store others' discoveries in your notebook for later attempts at new techniques.

Hand drawn

Hand drawn lines have energy. The speed of drawing the lines, the surface qualities, the shape of nib or brush, and the pressure applied during writing all combine to produce the quality of the characters. Calligraphic art is the expression of these forces, and successful calligraphy is that which appears free and without physical restraints. Speedily created lines have a smoother and more energetic curve than carefully plotted lines.

Transformation
The letters (*below*) were copied using a felt tip pen for an earlier pen mark alphabet. You can achieve interesting designs by converting one way of producing the letters into another.

Graffiti
The broad sweep of an arm (*above*), working on vertical surfaces, produces shapes which are quite unlike those made by a hand working on horizontal surfaces. Without the guiding control of the hand touching the surface the lines are often freer and more expressive.

Handwriting
The artist's use of handwriting to convey his message (*below*) is made more interesting because his style lacks the free confident expression of an adult, but contains some unsure and hesitant forms of a child practicing writing exercises.

Shape versus sense
Simplicity is not easy. The Viennese designer Alfred Roller may have had to draw out the word SECESSION (*left*) over and over again, exploring the combination of curves and linking lines until he arrived at a satisfactory solution. Then he may have had to experiment with the writing tool to achieve an even flowing line.

Tools
The alphabet (*top right*) is by designer Roger Kohn, who has injected humor and frivolity into his pen line alphabet. Although the letters do not have a common structure pattern, they belong together as a family because of their scratchy and witty shapes.

Surfaces
This alphabet (*right*) exploits the effect of thin paint on canvas. The surface texture is used to give the letters character and they all contain a strong dark part, reminiscent of beginning with a paint laden brush.

Task
Handwriting
Make a collection of written examples, and if possible enlarge words on a photocopier so that you can study the character of the curves.

Typographic forms
Although the letters in the 1967 poster (*below left*) by the designers Z Sklemer and J Mracek have their origins in normal printing letterforms, the designers have adapted and modified the shapes by personalizing each letter. These solutions are normally created with a pencil, then painted carefully with a brush.

Brush styles
The designer Hans Rudi Erdt has devised (*below*) in 1914 from the writing styles of German schoolbooks a continuous cursive form, which he has then exaggerated to produce lines of copy that flow like copious thick paint lines.

© DIAGRAM

Cut out

Just as a pen or a brush makes characteristic marks, so a knife or tearing will produce distinctive edges to the forms. It is most important that to produce the most effective and natural shape you should create the letterforms without first drafting out the shape in pencil. The freedom of the shapes will be more successful and spontaneous if you have imagined them while you are handling the knife, scissors or other tool.

Spaces are the message
The German artist who produced this design (*right*) cut the spaces from black card to reveal the shape of the letters. This method requires you to work out a provisional design, maybe with a broad-tipped pen. The final design is then made, referring to the provisional design from time to time.

1 *ABCDEFGHIJK NOPQRS*

2 ABCDEFGHIJKLMN

3 ABCDEFGHIJKLM

4 ABCDEFGHIJK LMNOPQ

SOIS JEUNE ET TAIS TOI

Crude need not be bad
The poster (*left*) was made by Paris students in 1968. The letters are cut out of silk screen stencil sheets and are then printed. Each letter is individual, but the total effect of the words is one of natural and free shapes.

Four methods
1 These letters, derived from dry transfer sheets or typesetters' specimen books, are cut up to produce dramatic effects.
2 Each letter is torn from gray paper.
3 The letters are cut from linoleum and printed.
4 The stencil is cut out of card and shown placed over black paper.

**LM
TUVWXYZ**

OPQRSTUVWXYZ

NOPQRSTUVWXYZ

RSTUVWXYZ

Dry transfer

The process of rubbing-down individual letters from sheets of alphabets provides the designer with great flexibility. The manufacturers offer hundreds of different varieties of letterforms in many different sizes and weights. As a method of exploring your ideas and of producing clean artwork, the dry transfer technique saves you time and extends your abilities. You have complete control of your design, but are not limited to your ability to form the shapes of the letters.

1 MORT MORT MORT MORT

2 montbanc

3 GOLIN

4 mozart

5 caRNiVaL

6 RASPUTIN

1 Letter spacing
The individually applied letters enable you to adjust the spacing either by opening out the letters or having them very close. You can also overlap the letters.

2 Alignment
Normal typography and lettering places all the letters on a common baseline – they are aligned. Dry transfer permits you to step up or down the horizontal positions of the letters.

3 Interlocking
Normally, each letter occupies its own space and the gaps between letters are usually constant. Dry transfer allows you to interlock the letters into one another's space.

4 Mixtures
You can use two sheets of letters of the same style and size but two different weights. This technique would be very difficult using any other method.

5 Varieties
Using a mixture of dry transfer sheets you can assemble words from a variety of sizes, styles and weights.

6 Transposition
By working on clear plastic film, and applying the letters to either side you can produce words with transposed letters.

7 Negative
The manufacturers produce dry transfer letters in a variety of colors as well as black and white. This enables you to apply the letters to dark or textured backgrounds. This solution has the letters applied to a pencil-rubbing of coarse texture.

7

8 Interference
By working with large letters, and putting these onto clear, smooth plastic film, you can subsequently scratch off the transfer material to create dynamic and expressive designs.

9 Curved
Because the letters are individually applied you can curve the direction of the baseline to suit your needs. This is particularly useful in simple mapping tasks.

10 Invention
You need not simply use the letters provided. You can adapt them to express your ideas. The word NEON was made by placing down the N and the E, then a letter C followed by a gap and then a back to front C. The word was ended with an N. The two Cs were then joined together using an inking pen and a brush.

11 Contrast
The letters in dry transfer alphabets are very carefully and accurately produced. You can exploit this feature and add hand work.

12 Distortion
Dry transfer can be applied to surfaces which are subsequently crumbled, torn or worn so that their textures become a feature of the letters.

13 Substitution
You need not only use the alphabet letters. Interesting ideas can be expressed by inserting other elements into the words.

Stencil

Stencil letters derive their form from the practice of pressing ink or paint through cut out holes in a surface. The letter-shaped holes must not be so large that they weaken the surface, and not too close to the other holes. The holes are separated by "bridges" of material which keep them in shape. The letters produced in this way have a characteristic shape which has been copied by designers producing new letterforms.

Task
Stencil styles
Using a fiber-tip pen, design an alphabet which resembles a stencil style (*right*). Make sure all letter elements are independent of each other and that the white "bridges" are of consistent thickness throughout. Try to think of each letter as having similar features.

Drafting stencils
The alphabet (*right*) is formed by holes in a sheet of plastic. These are used by architects to produce quick evenly-written labels for their drawings. The sample here has the lower case letters upside-down because the letters are formed by turning the stencil over and working from the other side.

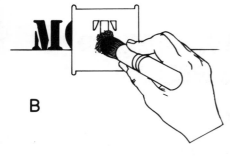

A

B

Stencils
These are either rows of letters (**A**) of a size which enables you to outline the shapes with a technical pen, or individual letters (**B**) large enough to allow you to brush-stencil the shapes.

Variety
The examples (*right*) show how varied the shapes of stencil letters can be, although all conform to the requirements of stencils. Some are dry-transfer alphabets in the style of stencil alphabets. The bottom alphabet is by the designer Edward Wright and is intended to be cast in metal or concrete for use on sign boards and plaques.

abcdefghijklmnc

ABCDEFGHIJK

äıdcefgjhikm

ÄBCDEGHJK

abcdefghijklm

ABCDEFCHIJKLM

ABCDEFGHIJKLM

ABCDEFGHIJKL

ABCDEGLANO SV
PUV Y AN WKAN

ßẞ×wvüſſſrpbⱸⱺuwwⱺbdıſſnʌmⱱⱶſſ

HJKLMN.ÖPRSTÜVWXYZ

pqrstuvwxyz

MNOPQRSTUVWXYZ

nöcprstvwxyz
MNÖPQRSTÜVWXYZ

opqrfsstuvwxyz

NOPQRESTU

OPQRSTUVWXYZ

MNOPQRSTUVWXYZ

New techniques

There is no such thing as a "correct" letterform — only those forms which tradition acknowledges as being more commonly in use. This diversity of forms will, in the future, be exploited to a far greater degree. Modern technology has the facility to change shapes electronically and photographically. Designers are constantly seeking new ways to express ideas (although many are simply old ideas which have been rediscovered). The computer-generated forms open up a vast array of opportunities for distortions and applications.

Spacing Spacing Spacing

Character spacing
One of the simplest methods of altering the appearance of a word is to adjust the character spacing (*above*). This can very easily be achieved with the modern technology of photosetting.

Deliberate accidents
The word "Sandberg" (*left*) was produced with dry transfer letters put onto card. The student then moved, twisted or raised the card while taking photocopies. Each accidental design leads the designer into thinking of applications for this form of photographic distortion.

Task
Photocopying
If you can gain access to a photocopying machine, place one of your earlier designs on the exposure bed. While the camera is operating, gently slide the original slightly across the plate. A great variety of distortions can be produced in this way.

Distortion
Distortion
Distortion

Character distortion
The word "Distortion" (*above*) kept its original typographical shapes, but was made to slope using digital electronic technology. These new techniques, although appearing to resemble traditional distorted forms, are in fact simple mathematical products and can often have discordant elements, for example the curve of the capital D.

Photography
The Italian designer Franco Grignani has used photographic methods to create this 1970s design. Not only do the words overlap, but many appear back to front. This technique would be extremely time consuming if it were produced by any method other than photography.

FASHION 500% exp.
FASHION 490% exp.
FASHION 480% exp.
FASHION 470% exp.
FASHION 460% exp.
FASHION 450% exp.
FASHION 440% exp.
FASHION 430% exp.
FASHION 420% exp.
FASHION 410% exp.
FASHION 400% exp.
FASHION 390% exp.
FASHION 380% exp.
FASHION 370% exp.
FASHION 360% exp.
FASHION 350% exp.
FASHION 330% exp.
FASHION 330% exp.
FASHION 320% exp.
FASHION 310% exp.
FASHION 300% exp.
FASHION 290% exp.
FASHION 280% exp.
FASHION 270% exp.
FASHION 260% exp.
FASHION 250% exp.
FASHION 240% exp.
FASHION 230% exp.
FASHION 220% exp.
FASHION 210% exp.
FASHION 200% exp.
FASHION 190% exp.
FASHION 180% exp.
FASHION 170% exp.
FASHION 160% exp.
FASHION 150% exp.
FASHION 140% exp.
FASHION 130% exp.
FASHION 120% exp.
FASHION 110% exp.
FASHION 100% normal
FASHION 10% cond.
FASHION 20% cond.
FASHION 30% cond.
FASHION 40% cond.
FASHION 50% cond.

New technology
The word "FASHION" (*left*) appears in its original height, style and weight as the 6th line from the bottom. All others are electronically distorted along the horizontal axis. Modern photosetting companies can offer the designer an infinite variety of distortion techniques.

Review

Ideas have legs! They jump out at you in the most unexpected ways. When faced with a design problem, your most successful solution may be the very first idea that occurs to you, or the last. Always have an open mind and try to bring fresh and new ideas to the problem. To help you achieve this, I have made a short list (it could be much longer!) of starting points, from which you can explore the features of your task. Never feel ashamed of using the solutions found by other designers – copying examples is the quickest way of gaining confidence in your own ideas. Remember that good solutions are often the simplest. DO NOT TRY TO BE CLEVER . . . only to become obscure. Legibility should be the primary concern of any statement. A brilliant design which is confusing and difficult to read will not succeed. Most of all, have fun. Creation is a wonderful activity, and, although sometimes difficult, it is very rewarding.

How to improve your design solution

Change its shape	**Change how you make it**	**Change its character**	**Change its position**
Flatten it	Typeset it	Do it in capitals	Do it upside down
Fatten it	Dry transfer it	Do it in lower case	Do it at the edge of the area
Thin it	Brush letter it	Do it in Italic	Do it at the top
Squeeze it	Use a quill	Do it in bold	Do it at the bottom
Stretch it	Use compasses and rule	Do it in light	Do it at the side
Bend it	Use pencil, chalk or crayon	Do it in solid letters	Write it upward
Curve it	Photoset it	Do it in outline letters	Write it sideways
Squash it	Cut it out	Do it in textured letters	Write it backward
Overlap it	Tear it out	Do it in color	Write it diagonally
Twist it	Scratch it out	Do it in 3D	
Slope it forward	Make it out of clay, tin,	Do it normal	**Go wild**
Slope it backward	metal, wood, sand, or	(not a bad idea . . .)	Smudge it
Put it in a square	anything else you can find		Scratch on it
Put it in a circle			Tear it up
Put it in a triangle	**Change a part**		Cut it up
	Mix capitals and lower case		Insert wrong letters
	Mix bold and light		Simplify it!
	Mix normal and Italic		Substitute pictures
	Mix decorative with plain		Substitute symbols
	Mix the way you make it		Try your own ways of distorting it
			Do lots of these methods at the same time

©DIAGRAM

1898

1906

Evolution
Current design solutions are the result of years of refining and developing ideas. The company symbol for "PEPSI" (*left*) has undergone serious revisions and simplifications since it was first developed in 1898.

1950

1962

Task
Creation
Try any or all of these suggested methods of transforming your lettering. Use words from this book, or from a magazine, as the original.

1973